THE NATIONAL TRUST

Investigating The Eighteenth Century

By Alison Honey
Illustrated by Peter Stevenson
Contents

The Background

The eighteenth century was one of tremendous change in every area of life; from royalty to religion, from exploration to education, and from fashion to food. Social changes began to make their mark against a background of religious and political upheaval which had been shaped by the dramatic events of the previous century.

Republic or monarchy?

The years between 1700 and 1800 saw many changes in the relationship between the monarchs, Parliament, and the ordinary people of the Britain. In the middle of the seventeenth century civil war had taken place when the Royalists (supporters of the king) had fought the Parliamentarians (people who thought that the king should share more of his power with parliament). Both religion and power were at stake and religion mattered strongly in a way which is sometimes hard for us to understand today.

Charles I, king from 1625 to 1649, was very stubborn. He refused to share power with Parliament and, even when his armies had been beaten, he insisted that only God had the right to judge him. The Parliamentarians did not agree and they executed him in 1649. The leader of the Parliamentarians, Oliver Cromwell, then ruled the country with the army, but when he died in 1658 there was no one strong enough to continue with his style of government, which in any case had become unpopular. In 1660 Parliament invited Charles I's son, who had escaped to France, to come back to England as king.

Charles II knew that he could not make the same mistake as his father. He was prepared to accept a more modern monarchy in which he shared power with Parliament, which was now becoming split into two main groups. However, there was a big argument over religion: the powerful nobles and gentry had got Parliament to pass laws declaring that only Anglicans (members of the Church of England) could hold top jobs, and the others wanted to go further and pass a law to stop the heir to the throne, Charles' Roman Catholic brother, James, becoming king. Charles II managed to have his way, and at his death in 1685, James II became king.

Charles I

Charles II

The Glorious Revolution

James II was quite popular – until he started to make changes which seemed to give the monarchy more power. He wanted a full-time army and gave positions of authority in both the army and government to Catholics, ignoring the laws which had been passed to stop Catholics holding high offices. This worried many different groups: if he wanted to, James could crush Parliament with his army and rule the country by himself. The one thing that consoled them was that James's two children, Mary and Anne – from his first marriage – were Anglicans, so when he died at least a Protestant would succeed to the throne.

Then disaster struck. In 1688, James's second wife gave birth to a son. The strong anti-Catholic group decided to act to prevent a new line of Catholic kings. They saw allies in James's daughter, Mary, and her husband, the Protestant Dutch ruler, William of Orange. He was persuaded to invade England with an army and take the throne from James II. Realising he had no support, James fled the country leaving William and Mary to become joint monarchs. This was known as the Glorious Revolution. The aristocrats and gentry thought that they had succeeded in recovering the Protestant line of succession, but more trouble lurked around the corner ...

The Last of the Stuarts

William and Mary had no children, so Mary's younger sister Anne was their heir. When Queen Anne came to the throne in 1702 she was to be the last of the Stuart family to reign over Britain. Although she gave birth to eleven children, none of them reached adulthood, so there was no direct heir to the throne when she died. The only other members of the Stuart family were her half-brother, James Edward, and his sister, but they were Catholics. After James II had fled in 1688, laws were passed saying that no Catholic could ever hold the throne of Britain again. That is still the case today.

The House of Hanover

The option was to trace the line through another more distant branch of the Stuart royal family. James I's grand-daughter, Sophia, had married a German prince, the Elector of Hanover. She was a Protestant. Parliament passed an Act in 1701 saying that the throne should pass to Sophia and her descendants on Queen Anne's death, to ensure that Protestants retained the crown. Sophia made an effort to learn English in preparation for her duties as queen, but died suddenly in 1714, only a couple of months before Anne died. Sophia's son, George, was left as the heir to the British throne.

This was the start of the House of Hanover; the next four kings were all to be called George and so – not surprisingly – the period from 1714 to 1830 is known as the Georgian age.

James II flees from William of Orange

Oliver Cromwell

3

Kings, Queens and also-rans

The first prime minister

When George I came to the throne there was a major stumbling block in his relationship with his chief ministers as he couldn't understand English. He didn't know what was going on so couldn't participate in regular meetings with ministers. Although he went to weekly meetings for three years, he gave up in 1717, and left matters in the hands of one person, Robert Walpole, the first Prime Minister. The Cabinet would discuss matters, come to an agreement, and Walpole would then go and tell the king what had been decided.

George I (1714-1727)

His heart was in Germany rather than Britain. He brought his own German favourites over with him: in particular, two women nicknamed 'the Maypole' and 'the Elephant and Castle'. Can you guess why they were called this? He had an unhappy marriage and had imprisoned his wife in Germany because she had taken a lover. He had little time for his eldest son who became ...

Queen Anne (1702-14)

The last of the Stuart royal family, Anne suffered badly from gout. She had a particularly bad attack on the day of her coronation in 1702 and had to be carried into Westminster Abbey in a sedan chair. The search for a Protestant heir to the throne ended eventually with

Walpole and George I discussing matters

George II (1727-1760)

'It is reported that his Hanoverian Majesty designs to visit his British dominion for three months in the spring.' Like his father, George II had mistresses and spent much of his time in Germany. But he also led Britain into battle against France which did much for his popularity. George II and his wife Caroline never liked their eldest son and heir, Prince Frederick. Queen Caroline once said

'Our first-born is the greatest ass, the greatest liar, the greatest canaille (scoundrel) and the greatest beast in the whole world and we heartily wish he was out of it.' Her wish was answered in 1751 when he was killed from a blow to the head by a tennis ball. Frederick's son came to the throne as ...

And finally ...
Bonnie Prince Charlie

In 1745 Charles Edward Stuart, a grandson of James II, known as Bonnie Prince Charlie, led a rebellion to seize what he saw as his rightful crown. His followers were called Jacobites, from the Latin form of James, the name of his father and grandfather. Most of his support lay in Scotland. With his supporters he drove George II's troops out of Scotland and marched down to Derby, but he realised he was not going to get enough support from the English and so decided to turn back northward. The Hanoverian army, led by George II's younger son, William, Duke of Cumberland, chased the fleeing rebels into Scotland and caught up with them at the battle of Culloden. The Jacobites were so brutally slaughtered that the Duke was known as 'Butcher' Cumberland from then onwards.

But these were not the only developments in the eighteenth century. The empire was expanding, changes in agriculture and industry were taking place, life in rural areas and cities was altering rapidly, and taste in everything from furniture, to food and fashion, was changing ...

George III (1760-1820)

Known as 'Farmer George' because he loved the countryside and was interested in agriculture. He was generally popular and was the first of the Georgian kings to be born in England and to speak English as his first language. He tried unsuccessfully to win some of the power of the monarchy back from Parliament. Later in his long reign he suffered from three bouts of madness, when he was declared unfit to rule and his son, the Prince Regent, had to take over temporarily. Some said that the madness was linked to lead poisoning from the jars which held his favourite foods of sauerkraut and lemonade. This is how one contemporary described the King's illness:

'November 11th 1788: The King is gravely ill in his mind, taken first with mental seizures and hallucinations last month when he attempted to shake hands with an oak tree in Windsor Park, declaring it to be his kinsman Frederick of Prussia.'

Country Life

'Turnip' Townshend

Turnips were found to be particularly good for putting the goodness back into the soil and could also be stored for feeding to livestock during the winter – one of the leading agricultural reformers, Lord Townshend, became nicknamed 'Turnip' Townshend for his enthusiasm over this crop. This meant that large numbers of animals no longer had to be killed and more and better quality fresh meat was available all year round, resulting in a huge difference in people's diet. In 1782, the record books at Shugborough in Staffordshire show that the chef was able to give everyone at least 1½lb of meat every day, as Lord Anson's model farm was producing large amounts of high-quality produce.

Life in the countryside saw major changes during the Georgian period. Landlords, keen to add to their wealth, invested money in improving their estates and encouraging their tenants to try new farming methods. They enclosed (fenced off for private use) land that had previously been held 'in common' by the community. They were careful to grow a variety of crops in rotation which meant the soil did not get exhausted and fields did not have to lie 'fallow' (empty) for a year to recover.

Jethro Tull

Developments in farming machinery led to greater efficiency. Jethro Tull invented a seed drill which meant that crops could be sown without waste and in straight lines, making them easier to weed. Agricultural shows were held around the country so that farmers could discuss ideas and methods. Arthur Young was a great agricultural enthusiast who spent much of his time travelling the country and writing down his impressions; this is his opinion of the estates of Lord Scarsdale, the owner of Kedleston Hall in Derbyshire, written in 1771:

'Lands that were so wet as to be almost boggy are by draining converted into excellent pasture; various other tracts of a barren quality are now improved to the utmost, so that you nowhere see any land that is not cloaked in a fine verdure [grass].'

The improvements spread across the whole country. In 1773, Theresa Parker, the mistress of Saltram House in Devon, wrote to her brother describing what had been taking place on their estate:

'amongst the many improvements you will find at this place those in farming are none of the least. The whole Down that you may remember between Boringdon and Cann Quarry, besides 200 acres of the same sort of furze Brake, is now covered with all sorts of corn, and affords a prospect of Plenty that is really very striking.'

A visitor to the Penrhyn Estate in Wales, writing in 1832, saw a huge difference in the appearance of the estate owned by the Pennant family:

'About forty years ago this part of the country bore a most wild, barren, and uncultivated appearance, but it is now covered with handsome villas, well built farm houses, neat cottages, rich meadows, well-cultivated fields, and flourishing plantations; bridges have been built, new roads made, bogs and swampy grounds drained and cultivated, neat fences raised, and barren rocks covered with woods. In fact, what has been accomplished in this neighbourhood in so short a space of time may be denominated a new creation, and that principally by means of one active and noble-minded individual who disposed of his vast resources in various acts of improvement; and by doing so gave employment to hundreds of his fellow-creatures, who were thus rendered comfortable and happy.'

Although these sort of improvements could often provide work for local people, as in the case of Penrhyn, more often than not the changes in the way estates were organised had a terrible effect on many of the very poor people living in the country. Most parishes had common ground on which anyone could graze animals and grow a few vegetables for their own use, but with the onset of enclosures, people who had no land of their own suddenly found themselves unable to produce enough food to survive. With the development of various kinds of labour-saving agricultural machinery many farm labourers found themselves out of a job and they were forced to move to the cities to find work in factories.

The changes in agriculture, known as the Agrarian Revolution, happened alongside developments in industry and manufacture known as the Industrial Revolution (see page 8). At the same time as farm labourers were being put out of work by the changes in agriculture, other members of the rural community also found their means of

living being taken away. Up to the last quarter of the eighteenth century, spinning and weaving had been done at home by hand by women and children. As machines to make cloth were invented, so the industry was shifted to huge new mills powered by water or steam. If people wanted a job they had to go where the work was, to the mills and the factories in fast-growing towns and cities, where they faced a very different lifestyle.

Industry

One of the greatest changes during the eighteenth century was in cloth production. Previously, most of the spinning and weaving work had been done by hand in country labourers' homes to produce cloth for merchants to sell. A revolution took place in the middle of the eighteenth century when machines were developed that could spin and weave very quickly. As the demand for cloth grew, mills and factories were set up. Machines were worked by waterpower, but by 1840 nearly all textile mills were powered by steam.

Quarry Bank Mill

Quarry Bank Mill in Cheshire was the brainchild of Samuel Greg. When Greg established his cotton mill the machines were powered by a water-wheels, so he had to chose a site on a river with a fast flowing current. He chose a spot on the River Bollin in the countryside outside Manchester, and in 1784 Quarry Bank Mill was ready to start producing cloth.

As steam power developed and factories were established in towns there was no difficulty finding people to work the machines but the early textile mills, like Quarry Bank, were usually situated in the heart of the country. One way around the problem was to employ 'pauper children' as apprentices – these were poor abandoned children, cared for by the local parish. In the late eighteenth century funds for looking after the poor became overstretched, as so many families were losing their homes and looking to the parish for support. The parish commissioners were very keen to pass the responsibility for pauper children to mill owners. Samuel Greg insisted that each child he took on came to him with a new set of clothing; in

return he promised the Parish that he would give 'sufficient Meat, Drink, Apparel [clothing], Lodging, Washing, and other Things necessary and fit for an Apprentice'.

The advantage of employing children was that they were cheap and small enough to crawl under the weaving machinery to free tangles. This was very dangerous work and the machines would still be working while the children tried to sort out jams, which meant there were many accidents. This is the description one apprentice gave of a mill accident:

'There was a great deal of cotton in the machine, one of the wheels caught my finger and tore it off, it was the forefinger of my left hand. I was attended by the surgeon of the factory Mr Holland and in about six weeks I recovered.'

The Penrhyn Slate Works

At the Penrhyn Estate in North Wales, the technical advances of the eighteenth century affected the slate industry, in existence in the area since the fifteenth century. Machinery didn't make that much difference to the job of the slate quarrymen, so the major change was the way in which the industry was organised and how slate was transported from the quarry.

Most of the improvements were put in place by Richard Pennant who inherited the estate in 1781 and also owned profitable sugar plantations in the West Indies (see page 16). Until Pennant took things in hand the slates were just used for building and roofing locally, the roads being too bad to transport the slates out in any quantity. Pennant built new roads from the quarry to the mouth of a river where he set up a port, Port Penrhyn, so that the slate could be carried down the mountain by cart and then loaded on to boats to be shipped to other parts of the country.

Richard Pennant built up very good contacts in the architectural and building world for selling his slates. He also realised that with the growing number of schools that there was a big market for blackboards and writing slates. He set up a small factory at Port Penrhyn which produced 136,000 writing slates every year.

The Penrhyn slate quarry is still working. It employs nearly 400 people and produces 500,000 tons of slate a year, including 30,000 tons of roofing slates – about one-sixth of the world's production.

Slate Quarrying

Richard Pennant

The child workers at Quarry Bank Mill lived together in the Apprentice House. And although they worked thirteen hours a day, six days a week they were treated fairly well compared with child workers at other mills. They were given meat to eat three times a week and fresh fruit and vegetables were grown in the Apprentice House garden.

Writing Slate

City Life

'*You stop and bump – porter runs against your shoulder. "By your leave", after he has knocked you down. In the road itself chaise after chaise, coach after coach, cart after cart. Through all this din and clamour, and the noise of thousands of tongues and feet, you hear the bells from the church-steeples, postmen's bells, the street-organs, fiddles and tambourines of itinerant musicians, and the cries of the vendors of hot and cold food at the street corners. A rocket blazes up stories high amidst a yelling crown of beggars, sailors and urchins. Some one shouts "Stop, thief", his handkerchief is gone. Every one runs and presses forward, some less concerned to catch the thief than to steal a watch or purse for themselves*'.

Georg Christoph Lichtenburg, *Visits to England*

That was a description of London by a German visitor in the 1770s showing that the city was a chaotic, noisy and dangerous place. Even so, many improvements had been made to the city of London in the mid-eighteenth century, such as the pavements introduced after the 1762 Paving Act. Until then, carriages, pedestrians, sedan chairs and animals all jostled together on the street. Signs (like today's pub signs) used to hang above all shops but in the 1760s these were banned – from the following remark by a contemporary Londoner you can see why!

'*From almost every house an enormous sign was suspended, which darkened the street, often fell down, and sometimes killed people*'.

Crime and punishment

There was a great deal of crime in the cities and no effective way of controlling it. Highwaymen even lurked in the centre of London ready to rob the coaches of the rich returning to their town houses. Fanny, the wife of Admiral Edward Boscawen of Hatchlands, wrote in January 1748, to tell him of the recent crime wave in Mayfair:

'*But you will see from the papers that notre quartier (our area) is come into great disgrace, there having been a robbery over against our chapel, by highwaymen on horseback. There have been two since in Grosvenor Square, but they have not been half so much talked about as ours, which, being the first, surprised the more, and the loss was much the greatest, a West Indian woman and her daughter losing jewels to the value of £400*'.

For serious offences the punishment could be death by public hanging which was meant to put people off committing crimes. But the public executions tended to be turned into a sort of grisly entertainment, where huge crowds gathered to cheer the prisoner to the scaffold. A common punishment for fairly minor crimes was transportation to the colonies; initially to America and then to Australia – a big price to pay.

ye Picke Pocket

Mother's ruin

The middle of the eighteenth century saw a huge increase in the drinking of gin. By 1743 people were drinking six times as much as they had in 1700. The reason was that gin is made from grain, and the grain harvests had been so good that there was a surplus to make gin with and no licence was needed to sell it. The poor often spent what money they had on spirits leading to a big alcoholism problem. Towns were crowded with gin shops whose slogan was 'Drunk for a penny, dead drunk for tuppence'.

A place in the town

Alongside this grim side of city life, the wealthy led an extravagant lifestyle. Many elegant town houses were built in the Georgian period, designed by top architects of the day such as Robert Adam, William Chambers and James Stuart. In London, squares like St James's and Bloomsbury were developed as highly fashionable residential areas and little expense was spared on building, even though often it was quite a challenge for the architect to build a grand house with suites for entertaining on a relatively small site.

The wealthy would also have country seats, dividing their time between fashionable London and the country. During the London 'season', huge parties or 'routs' would be held, and often a temporary extra room had to be put up at the back of the town house to make more space – although half of the fun of the party seemed to involve the guests being squashed together! This is one partygoer's description of a typical rout where he saw a:

'vast crowd of elegantly dressed ladies and gentlemen, many of whom are so over-powered by the heat, noise, confusion, as to be in danger of fainting. Everyone complains of the pressure of the company, yet all rejoice at being so divinely squeezed. The company moves from room to room; and the most an individual can do, on meeting a particular friend, is to shake hands as they are hurried past each other.'

Goede, *The Stranger in England*

The Joys of Travel

Although travelling today can be complicated by nose-to-tail traffic jams and rail strikes, at least we know that the roads and railways exist and that journeys are possible. In the early eighteenth century it was a very different story. Roads were often in a terrible condition: flooded and muddy in wet weather and rutted and dusty when it was dry.

Tolls and turnpikes

The eighteenth century brought great improvements in transport. Officially each parish was responsible for its roads but this was not an efficient system and many were neglected. Parliament passed laws to set up Turnpike Trusts which could buy stretches of road, charge a fee or 'toll' to people who travelled on them, and use the money for upkeep. Although some Trusts just pocketed the money and left the roads almost as bad as before, many others took their responsibility seriously and built new roads and bridges.

Travel was particularly difficult for women; men could ride off on a single horse with perhaps one servant, but it was expected that refined females should travel in a coach accompanied by a handful of attendants. This required a great deal more organisation, with fresh horses required for different stages of the journey. Travelling by coach was also much slower than on horseback; there was the ever-present danger of highwaymen who lurked on their fast horses ready to terrorise and rob passing travellers.

This is what Lady Anne Brownlow of Belton House, Lincolnshire, discovered when she investigated the possibilities of going to visit some relatives in Bedfordshire with her daughter, Jenny:

> *'upon inquiry about the roades, I find it is too hazardous. They assure me my own horses would not doe it, I find I must have six horses and two servants to ride bye. Jenny is sadly disappointed. I would send her with a servant in the Stage Coach & I daresay you could meet her at Huntingdon, but then I don't know how to get her to Hatley.'*

Carriages and cart horses

Carriages also improved during the eighteenth century – lighter and better sprung, making them more comfortable for long-distance travel. With these improvements people could come and go much more frequently.

Fear of phaetons

Phaetons were the lightest and fastest of the new carriages, the sports cars of the eighteenth century. In *Evelina*, a novel written by Fanny Burney in 1778, one of the older female characters reveals her suspicion of these rapid chariots, saying *'My will is yet unsigned, and I don't choose to venture in a phaeton with a young man while that is the case'*.

Slowcoach

The advances in travel weren't available to everyone and the poor had little option but to walk or travel in a stage waggon, a long cart pulled by eight carthorses. Although this method of travelling was very slow (only 2mph) – and uncomfortable – it was considered safe as highwaymen never bothered stopping stage waggons. Regularly running stage coaches appeared in the middle years of the century and were the equivalent of today's long-distance coaches. From London, it took two days to reach Bristol and ten to twelve days to travel to Edinburgh.

Stage Waggon

Amusements at home ...

During the eighteenth century travel to spa towns, to 'take the waters', became very popular. Bath was one city which flourished during Georgian times and much of its architecture dates from this time. In Bath, a flourishing spa, people not only took the waters, but also indulged in another popular activity, attending Assemblies. These were public gatherings where members of the gentry could dance, play cards, listen to music, eat or just talk to their friends and parade in their finery. At Kedleston, Adam and Curzon provided a 'mini-spa' for visitors, which included a bath-house and hotel.

Taking the waters at Bath

... and abroad

Although it was traditional for wealthy young men to travel abroad as part of their education on the Grand Tour (see page 22), with improvements in transport it was becoming easier for anyone who had the time and money to cross the Channel and see the wonders of the Continent.

In 1784 four young women left England for a trip which was to last ten years. Jane Parminter, her sister Elizabeth, their cousin Mary and a friend, Miss Colville, travelled through France, Italy, Germany, Switzerland, Spain and Portugal to see the sights. Unfortunately Jane only kept her diary for the first two months of the trip but from that you can see the sort of

things which eighteenth-century tourists would have visited and descriptions of the places where they stayed. They didn't like Paris and stayed in *'a very dirty inn indeed, the staircase shaking, the maids bold and impertinent'*, but things looked up when they visited the royal palace of Versailles and spotted Louis XVI and his Queen, Marie Antoinette.

Although Louis XVI was one of the most powerful men at the time, Jane, was not very impressed and described him as *'a corpulent man not strikingly agreeable'*. She was more taken with the Royal Menagerie (a sort of private zoo) where she saw *'the buffalo, the rhinoceros, the Pelicans, African sheep with no tail and a great variety of other things.'*

13

Exploration and Discovery

A voyage round the world

Conflict was one of the main reasons for much world travel in the eighteenth century. In 1739 war broke out between Spain and England. It was called rather strangely 'The War of Jenkin's Ear'. Robert Jenkins had been in command of a merchant ship sailing peacefully back to England from the West Indies which was stopped and searched by a Spanish customs officer, and some of its cargo confiscated. In the scuffle Jenkin's ear was cut off and he kept the grisly souvenir as evidence of his unjust and violent treatment at the hands of the Spanish. By the end of the 1730s, tensions were running high between Spain and England and Jenkin's ear was used as an excuse to spark off a war.

The Prime Minister Robert Walpole was very reluctant to fight as he knew that war was expensive, but public opinion was too strong and open warfare was declared. Walpole's fears came true and the 'War of Jenkin's Ear' got drawn into the larger European conflict called the Wars of Austrian Succession. The British Government decided that one of the best ways to hurt the Spanish was to cut off supplies of treasure from their colonies.

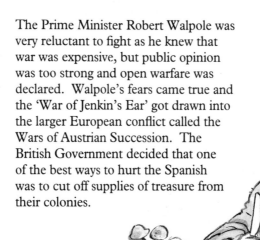

Admiral Anson

George Anson, an experienced naval officer, was chosen as the commander of a squadron of five ships to sail to the south seas to harass Spanish ships and, if possible, capture the Spanish treasure galleon carrying silver and other riches from the South American colonies. He was given the option of coming back via China and completing the circuit round the world. Sir Francis Drake had been the only Englishman to do this two hundred years earlier.

The chaplain, Rev. Richard Walter, on Anson's ship, *Centurion*, kept a diary of the voyage. After their safe return home his writings were published and became a best seller. It is hard to imagine the sort of conditions which sailors put up with on expeditions like this. After a few days at sea all the supplies of fresh food were used up and the crew had to eat dried biscuits, which as the weeks went by were eaten up by insects called weevils. However, people didn't seem to expect much from the food or drink judging from comments made by Rev. Walter about the water from the island of Santa Catherina off the Brazilian coast:

> 'The water is excellent, and preserves at sea as well as that of the Thames. For after it has been in the cask a day or two it begins to purge itself, and stinks most intolerably, and is soon covered with a green scum. But this in a few days sinks to the bottom, and leaves the water as clear as crystal, and perfectly sweet.'

Anson at the Admiralty

George Anson is known as the Father of the British Navy. After his epic journey he was promoted to work at the Admiralty on naval reforms. He recognised the importance of clean conditions on board and that fresh fruit and vegetables helped combat scurvy, the disease that commonly attacked sailors. He also saw that uniform gave a sense of discipline and enabled sailors to distinguish rank. He improved techniques in boat building, introducing copper bottoms on which barnacles could not grow and rot the timbers. His work at the Admiralty set the foundations for a very efficient British navy.

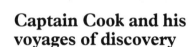

George Anson & Centurion

Anson left England with five ships but returned with only his own, the *Centurion*. Most of the problems were due to the horrendous weather conditions, disease, and the fact that navigation in those days was still very hit and miss and the ships were often hundreds of miles off course.

Somehow Anson succeeded in sticking to his mission and caught several smaller Spanish ships, reached China and – most importantly – seized the huge prize of the Spanish galleon with its £400,000 of treasure on board. In the short battle to capture the galleon the *Centurion* lost only three men while 67 Spanish sailors were killed and 84 wounded. Anson, and what remained of his original squadron, returned home via Indonesia and the Cape of Good Hope.

The expedition almost ended in disaster. On the very last leg of the voyage up the English Channel the *Centurion* sailed through the middle of a fleet of French warships but, thanks to the thick fog, the ship was not noticed, and after three years and nine months the *Centurion* landed on home shores again.

The Cat Monument, Shugborough

Home improvements

Anson's family home was at Shugborough in Staffordshire. His successful voyage round the world brought fame and riches to the family, enabling great building and landscape improvements to take place. One of the monuments in the garden features a cat sitting on top of an urn. Some say that it is dedicated to a cat that accompanied Admiral Anson on his journey.

Captain Cook

Captain Cook and his voyages of discovery

Twenty-four years after Anson's voyage round the world, Captain James Cook set off on a very different sort of trip. His mission was to explore the Pacific and chart the new lands he found. He had a team of artists and scientists aboard to draw and study plants and animals unknown in Europe. His first voyage in 1768 took him to Tahiti, New Zealand, Australia and other Pacific islands and he brought back records of strange animals like kangaroos as well as tales of cannibals. Cook had learnt by Anson's experience that fresh supplies were essential on a long trip. He set sail with live hens, sheep and pigs which were killed as necessary, as well as large amounts of pickled cabbage and onions.

Sugar and Slavery

During the seventeenth century the islands of the West Indies became the centre for producing and exporting sugar and its by-products, molasses and rum, for the European market. Unfortunately this desire for sugar promoted one of the most horrible aspects of the eighteenth century – the slave trade.

Merchants realised that they could get very rich very easily by the so-called 'triangular trade'. They left England in ships laden with cheap goods and sailed to West Africa. Here they would buy Africans captured in tribal warfare, brand them like cattle, and cram the chained prisoners below decks ready for the next leg of the voyage to the West Indies.

The conditions on slave ships were indescribable and a quarter of the slaves died before even reaching the West Indies. If they survived the voyage they then faced the back-breaking labour of working on the sugar plantations. The work was so hard and the death rate so high that a constant supply of new slaves was needed. The last leg of the 'triangle' was the journey from the West Indies back to England when the ships carried the cargo of sugar, molasses and rum to be sold at a high price to buyers in ports like Liverpool and Bristol.

Due to the growing demand for sugar in Europe, combined with the fact that the slave trade provided them with free labour the owners of the sugar plantations were phenomenally rich. However, the climate and disease on the islands did not make them an attractive place to settle, and most owners moved back to Britain as soon as they could, leaving a manager in control. They were known as absentee landlords. The Pennant family of Penrhyn in North Wales had been one of the first British families to settle in the West Indies, when Gifford Pennant established a sugar plantation in Jamaica in 1658.

Gilbert Pennant's grandsons, John, Samuel and Henry, returned and settled in Britain, but kept in close touch with the running of the estate. Samuel became Lord Mayor of London but the theory that Britain was a healthier place than Jamaica collapsed in his case, when he died from 'jail-fever', caught from a prisoner in court!

The sugar trade made many families very wealthy. The Onslows of Clandon in Surrey were one such family. Thomas Onslow married the daughter of a well-known – and very rich – Jamaican family, and it was this West Indian wealth that enabled him to build Clandon Park in the 1730s.

Samuel Pennant catches jail-fever

The end of slavery

Towards the end of the eighteenth century some people were questioning the slave trade, and in 1787 William Wilberforce, a young MP and friend of the Prime Minister, William Pitt, started a society to campaign for its abolition. One of the images they used to appeal to people was a picture of a slave kneeling in chains with the slogan 'Am I not a man and a brother?'.

The plantation owners, including Richard Pennant, very unhappy at the prospect of losing their free labour, opposed the anti-slavery movement. Richard Pennant, MP for Liverpool, gave many speeches in Parliament defending the slave trade, becoming known as 'Chairman of the West Indian merchants'. But in 1807 the planters lost their battle and the slave trade was banned. It was not until 1833 that all slaves in the British Empire were freed and at that time there were 764 slaves working on the Pennant family's Jamaican estates. In compensation the Pennants received £14,683 – about £20 per slave.

How the sugar cane was processed

Sugar canes were cut down and taken to the sugar mill, where the juice was squeezed out through crushing them between rollers pulled by oxen (*these rollers were later powered by steam*). The liquid ran into huge copper pots and was boiled until it crystallised into sugar.

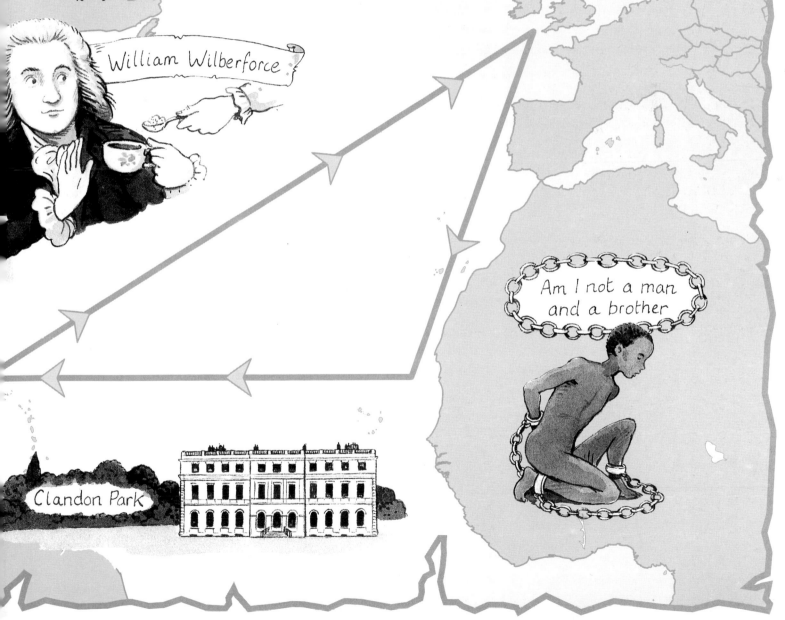

William Wilberforce

Am I not a man and a brother

Clandon Park

Classical Glory

'*The day was fine and we resolved to go by Kedleston, the seat of Lord Scarsdale, that I might see his Lordship's fine house. I was struck with the magnificence of the building, and the extensive park, covered with deer, cattle and sheep delighted me. The number of old oaks filled me with respectful admiration. The excellent smooth gravel roads, the large piece of water formed by his Lordship with a handsome barge upon it, the venerable church, now the chapel, just by the house, in short the grand group of objects agitated and distended my mind in a most agreeable manner.*'

This was the reaction of Dr Johnson in 1777 when he visited one of the finest houses to be built in the eighteenth century, Kedleston Hall, the home of the Curzon family in Derbyshire. The Curzons were very wealthy landowners, owning nearly 10,000 acres of land. Partly as a sign of his standing, and also to provide somewhere suitable to display his enormous collection of paintings and sculpture, Sir Nathaniel Curzon, who inherited the estate in 1758, lost no time in deciding to build a new house in the foremost style of the day. He also decided to re-landscape the grounds – and when we say re-landscaping, we *mean* re-landscaping; the whole village was moved to a new location outside the park walls. The ancient village church then became the chapel to the house containing family monuments and tombs. Sir Nathaniel even managed to get an Act of Parliament passed to divert the public road away from the front of the house!

The New Plan

Curzon had originally hired two architects; first Matthew Brettingham, followed by James Paine, to work on the new house. But in 1760 he decided to give the whole project over to the rising star, Robert Adam. Adam, from a family of Scottish architects, had spent much time abroad studying classical buildings and remains, to see how he could adapt them to use in his own designs.

During the eighteenth century the neo-classical style of architecture became extremely popular. 'Neo' means new, and is used to refer to a revival of an older style. This is what people were looking for – a link with what they viewed as the golden era of classical Greece and Rome. Adam was particularly impressed by Roman architecture and was nicknamed 'Bob the Roman' while James Stuart, another neo-classical designer, was influenced by Greek architecture, and was known as 'Athenian Stuart' after Athens, the capital of Greece.

Jack of all trades, master of all

Robert Adam was not only an architect – he provided a whole range of services for his clients. His projects were designed as a whole, with all the interior decoration, furniture and fittings – down to key holes – designed by him. He would choose the colour scheme, place each piece of furniture, and decide where to hang paintings. Adam provided a total design service, and expected the co-operation of his patron.

To undertake this work Adam drew on a network of highly skilled craftsmen who travelled all over the country profiting from the new interest in interior decoration. He was once described as being accompanied by 'a regiment of artificers'– an army of craftsmen! Adam kept very detailed account books, so it is easy to trace how much his various workers charged. On the opposite page you can see a page from the account books held at Kedleston showing the breakdown of the costs (in pounds, shillings and pence) for Sir Nathaniel Curzon's new house.

	£	s	d
Bricklayers	**2,685**	**12**	**0**
Masons *(Joseph Hall and Francis Battersby)*	6,596	1	0
Slaters *(Pratt & C0.)*	344	18	0
Glaziers *(Joseph Taylor and William Cobbett)*	477	10	11½
Copper Smith, etc, and skylight *(William Kinsman)*	307	0	0
Plumbers	1,354	4	6
Painter *(Thomas Smith)*	113	17	0
Carpenters/Joiners	5,104	8	0
Plasterers *(Abraham Denston [plain]* *Joseph Rose and Co. [decorative])*	1,520	12	0
Ironmongers & Smiths work	478	12	0
Carvers *(Joshua Hall and George Moneypenny)*	2,501	3	0
Chimney-pieces to 4 Rooms *(Joseph Pickford and Michael Spang)*	990	0	0

Sundries brought the total to   £22,508 9s 4¼d

Open to the public

From the start Curzon intended to show his new house to the public and one of the duties of his housekeeper, Mrs Garnett, was to show visitors round. There is a portrait at Kedleston showing her clutching a guidebook to the house. This is how she was described by James Boswell, who visited the house with Dr Johnson, in 1777:

'Our names were sent up, and a well-drest elderly Housekeeper, a most distinct Articulator, showed us the House …'

The average weekly wage of a farm labourer in 1760 was 5 shillings (25p), so the £22,500 plus spent by Curzon on his new house was enormous, especially when you realise that he would have spent additional amounts on the re-landscaping. Many of Adam's other clients, although keen to show their interest in his architectural ideas, would not have had so much money to spare or didn't want to go as far as Curzon in demolishing a perfectly good house just to build a more fashionable one. They chose to employ Adam to extend or remodel an existing house, or give a facelift to the interior decor.

Kedleston Hall

The Personal Touch

Robert Adam took great care over every detail. He redesigned the interiors of Hatchlands Park in Surrey in 1758, using a nautical theme on some of the ceilings, with patterns of mermaids, dolphins, sea-horses and anchors. There was a good reason for this – the owner of the house was Edward Boscawen, a famous Admiral who wanted to be reminded of the sea while living inland!

Return to Nature

During the eighteenth century there was a move away from the formal gardens of the sixteenth and seventeenth century to a more natural style. Many country house owners decided to dig up their parterres (flowers and hedges planted in complicated patterns), and their formal avenues, in order to replace them with lawns, lakes, huge expanses of grass and tree clumps in a parkland style. The idea was to make things look natural and unplanned – although in fact these landscapes were made entirely by people, with careful thought put into the placing of each tree!

In 1734, Thomas Robinson wrote about the new fashion to his friend Lord Carlisle:

The craze took hold rapidly, despite the huge expense which the owners had incurred in creating the formal gardens not so long ago.

'Mr Kent' was William Kent, a leading architect and landscape designer, who worked for many country house owners wanting to give their gardens a new look. Another aspect of the new fashion was to set small temple-like buildings into the landscape, and Kent made the design of garden buildings his speciality. The aim was to re-create a 'classical' landscape as a setting for the classical house.

Before

After

'A general alteration of some of the most considerable gardens in the Kingdom is begun after Mr Kent's notion, viz. to lay them out and work without level or line ... This method of gardening is the more agreeable as, when finished, it has the appearance of beautiful nature, and without being told, one would imagine art had no part in the finishing. The celebrated gardens of Claremont, Chiswick and Stowe are now full of labourers to modernise the expensive works finished in them even since everyone's memory.'

Doing the rounds

Many of the new-style gardens were designed as a circuit with routes taking visitors round the various garden buildings and showing off the different views. The gardens at Stowe in Buckinghamshire were some of the most famous of the time: by 1760 there were over thirty different garden buildings to visit. Some circuits were so long that carriages were needed to complete the trip.

Temple of British Worthies, designed by William Kent.

Sitting on the fence

It was difficult for landscape designers to strike the balance between the natural look and privacy. Clients (or patrons) liked the idea of seeing cows grazing outside the windows but were not so keen on the possibility of stepping in a cow pat. One designer, Charles Bridgeman, came up with a simple but effective solution: he dug a ditch between the lawns of the house and the parkland beyond, which meant animals couldn't get in but there was no fence to spoil the view. This became known as a ha-ha, after the surprised cry which people would let out when coming across the hidden barrier, 'Aha!'.

Some people wanted their grounds to be a sort of rural theme park with dairymaids and shepherd boys – but without any of the dirt! This is what Jemima, wife of the 2nd Earl of Hardwicke at Wimpole Hall in Cambridgeshire, wrote about the alterations to the grounds in 1753, joking that her:

'only objection to the modern improvements of gardens is their not encouraging shade enough or privacy ... At this moment there is a flock of sheep feeding upon the lawn under my window tended by a shepherd boy, who does not indeed pipe, but he sings all day or employs himself in erecting lime twigs to catch the harmless birds.'

NTPL / A C Cooper

Spot the difference

Humphrey Repton was another landscape designer who altered the grounds of a number of country houses in the late eighteenth and early nineteenth centuries. He put all his plans in a series of Red Books in which flaps covered the 'before' with the 'after' versions of the landscape.

His predecessor as the leading landscape designer of his day, Capability Brown, had made substantial to many estates, whereas Repton was more concerned with alterations within landscapes created by Brown, and brought a little more formality back to country house gardens. At Wimpole Hall in Cambridgeshire Repton made a series of recommendations which were not taken up, but his proposed changes can still be seen in his Red Book. Everything is carefully planned to look very natural!

The Arts

The Grand Tour

The seventeenth century had been an age when people were fascinated by science and really began to question how things worked. Between 1600 and 1750 scientific instruments were developed such as telescopes, microscopes and thermometers. But during the eighteenth century the interest shifted to the arts and classical history. The ancient civilisations of Rome and Greece were considered by many to be a golden era.

It was considered part of a young gentleman's education to spend a couple of years travelling abroad with his tutor visiting ancient sites, perhaps learning foreign languages and buying antiques and works of art – a sign of wealth and culture. Many of the travellers had their portraits painted by foreign artists such as the Italian, Pompeo Batoni. Usually the tutor would keep a record of expenses and we can learn from these account books how the money was spent on these trips.

In general, travel on the Continent became a lot easier, so that gentlemen who were really bitten by the travel bug, and by European art, could move to and fro without much difficulty, as long as they could afford it. One great traveller, the 4th Earl of Bristol, spent many years abroad and forked out thousands of pounds building up his art collection. He created Ickworth in Suffolk as a suitable setting for his art collections. This is his description of a spending spree in Amsterdam in 1790:

> *'My purchases three years ago from Mr. Hope of Amsterdam amounted in one morning to £3,000 and the next day I bought for £750 more'.*

Age of contrasts

Portrait painting was very popular during the eighteenth century and Britain produced some great artists, such as Sir Joshua Reynolds and Thomas Gainsborough. In 1768 George III founded the Royal Academy of Arts and Sir Joshua Reynolds was appointed as its first president.

Reynolds specialised in painting portraits of members of the aristocracy and he had a tremendous output. His dignified portraits showed off the sitter in the best light. He had the advantage of coming from a well-connected family and so was on an equal social footing with many of his subjects. The Parker family who lived at Saltram in Devon were particularly friendly with Sir Joshua and we know that John Parker, Lord Boringdon, asked him for advice on what artists to buy from or collect. Reynolds also painted at least ten portraits of members of the family; these paintings now hang at Saltram.

Another famous eighteenth century artist was William Hogarth. His approach to his subjects was very different from Reynolds. He was much more interested in putting across a message or story in his work, giving us much more of a feeling of what everyday life was like in the eighteenth century.

Hogarth's engraving, *Gin Lane*, illustrates the evils of the drink during the London Gin Craze (see page 11). You can see the chaos in the streets littered with drunk people. The woman at the centre of picture is too drunk to notice that her baby is falling over the steps, while on the right-hand side another woman pours a cup of gin down her baby's throat. In the background, outside a coffin maker's premises, a man, dead from drink, is being put into a casket, while in the bottom right corner a blind beggar has obviously spent all his money on drink and is starving. The first verse under the print read:

'Gin, cursed fiend, with Fury fraught, Makes human Race a Prey, It enters by a deadly draught and steals our Life away'.

No respect

Magazines such as the *Spectator* and *Tatler* published essays by leading writers like Alexander Pope and Joseph Addison making fun of people in authority. Nobody was safe from attack and there were many cartoons mocking the appearance and behaviour of different members of the royal family.

Blewcoat Boy

The Blewcoat School in Victoria, London, was built in 1709 and is now a National Trust shop. You can see the statue of the Blewcoat Boy in the niche on its outer wall. Sixty or so children went there from the surrounding slums to learn basic lessons to give them a better start in life. When it was first set up the school only accepted boys, but in 1713 the trustees decided to admit 20 girls as well.

Uniform was important; it helped to give a charity school child a sense of belonging, making him instantly recognisable in the streets to the people who'd contributed funds to the running of the school. In the district of Westminster there were three charity schools – the Greencoat, Greycoat and Blewcoat and it was easy to tell where a child went to school just by looking at the colour of his uniform.

A better start

40 pairs of shoes –	£4.00
40 coats with four dozen buttons –	£4.1s
40 pairs of stockings and gloves –	£4.10s
42 'capps' –	£1.19s
'Rails of peggs for their cloaths' –	6d
42 Bibles –	£4.18s

This is the setting-up bill for the uniforms and books for the first forty pupils of the Blewcoat School in 1709 – one of London's first 'charity schools'. Schooling in the eighteenth century was not compulsory and many children of the poorer classes were put out to work as young as possible. Even if the parents had wanted their children to go to school they would have had to pay and few would have had the money to spare. However, during the late seventeenth and early eighteenth centuries wealthy tradesmen all over the country took matters into their own hands and provided the funds to start up schools in poor areas, particularly in the cities. By financing the schools these benefactors aimed to give needy children a basic education in religion, reading and writing, and prepare them for entry as apprentices to a trade. By 1740 the idea had become so popular that there were nearly 2,000 charity schools in England.

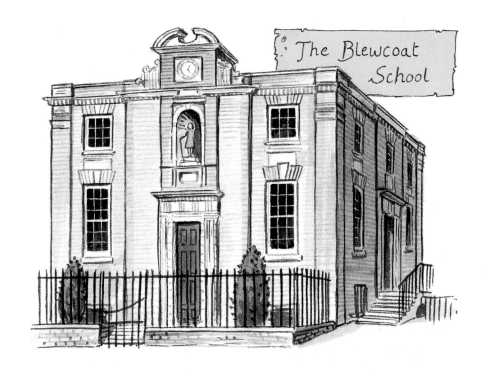

The Blewcoat School

Blewcoat Boy

In return for this free education parents had to accept strict rules and virtually hand over their children's future to the school. As the pupils came from very poor backgrounds the trustees made sure that the temptation of having good clothes and school books in the house was removed. Rules stated that parents were not allowed to *'keep any of their children's Books or Clothes at home … neither shall they embezzle, pawn or sell the same'.* It was also left up to the trustees to choose a suitable apprenticeship for each child when the time came to leave school. Blewcoat girls often trained as domestic servants, seamstresses and fan-makers, while the boys could be placed with Thames watermen and fishermen, joiners, tailors, bricklayers, coopers (barrel makers) and many other craftsmen to learn a trade.

Apprenticeship could often be a hard and cruel time and it was not uncommon for children to be treated like slaves – beaten, neglected and starved. To avoid this, the trustees of the charity schools did their best to investigate placements thoroughly before a child was handed over. As a further safeguard the master was only given part of the fee when he accepted the child, and the rest at the end of the year when both sides were satisfied that things were going well.

Public School pyromania

At the other end of the scale from charity schools were the public schools (or private boarding schools) which became more and more exclusive during the eighteenth century. When Harrow and Eton had been founded in the fifteenth century, they were for the sons of tradesmen and craftsmen, but by the eighteenth century most of the pupils were sons of gentlemen and aristocrats. In spite of this they were often quite lawless places and rebellions were not unusual – in 1797 pupils at Rugby ran riot, set fire to their desks and mined the headmaster's study with gunpowder!

All work and no play

The new textile factories and mills employed children as cheap labour (see Quarry Bank Mill, page 8). These child workers often had to work thirteen hours a day, six days a week and there was little opportunity for getting a basic education. In 1780 Sunday Schools were set up to cater for children in full time work, which meant that every day of the week was taken up by either work or study.

Food and Health

Entertaining in style

Wealthy people ate very well and entertained with little worry about expense. Sir Harry Fetherstonhaugh and his mother were hosts to a racing party at their home, Uppark in Sussex, in 1784. The Prince of Wales was present and so perhaps the quantity and quality of food was even more extravagant than usual. Lady Fetherstonhaugh had to estimate how much food and drink the hundred or so guests would consume and here are a few extracts from her shopping list and accounts:

'2 Bucks [deer], a Welsh sheep, a doz. Ducks, – 4 Hams, dozens of pigeons, and Rabbits, Flitches [sides] of Bacon, Lobsters and Prawns; a Turtle of 120 lbs.; 166 lbs. of Butter; 376 Eggs, 67 Chickens; 23 Pints of Cream, 30lbs. of Coffee, 10 lbs. of Fine Tea; and three lbs. of common tea.'

'41 Port; 7 Brandy; 1 ½ Hold of strong Beer; while Musick cost £26 5s 0d and another chef to assist Moget cost £25; another 2 Bucks added cost £11; 2 more sheep cost only £2 10s, and another 2 carp £1 10s 0d.'

Meanwhile ...

It was a very different story for the poor. Most labourers in the town and country ate a basic diet of bread and cheese with meat perhaps just once a week. In the country the poor could maybe add some home-grown vegetables to their diet. In London and other big cities, living conditions were often so cramped that there was little or no room to cook and many people relied on pie sellers and cook shops for their food.

A Georgian recipe

To Make a Potatoe-Pudding

'Take 12 oz of Potatoes pound them very fine in a Mortar [with] 12 Yolks of Eggs, 4 Whites, 12oz sugar, 12oz of butter, some Mace and Cynnamon dry'd and powdered – a Spoonful or two of Brandy, as much Citron as you please. A Quarter of an Hour will bake it, put it in puff paste – round the brim.'

From an eighteenth-century recipe book at Montacute

Tricks of the trade

White bread was very popular and bakers found several strange ways of making their bread whiter than white by adding lime, chalk and alum to the dough. One writer even accused bakers of grinding up human bones to make dazzling white bread.

Milkmen and women in towns also devised revolting tricks to make their milk look attractive to the unsuspecting customer – by squeezing the juice from snails and stirring it in, they made the milk look fresh and frothy.

Conquering smallpox

Bubonic plague devastated the population in the seventeenth century, killing 70,000 people in London in 1665. There were still several nasty diseases around to haunt people in the eighteenth century. The most feared of these was probably smallpox – it killed anyone regardless of how rich or poor they were and was very contagious. Throughout the century about three in five people caught smallpox and one in five died.

In 1796 a doctor, Edward Jenner, made a tremendous breakthrough – he'd noticed that milkmaids never got smallpox and worked out that there must be a link with cowpox, a common cattle disease. His theory was that by inoculating people with cowpox – a milder strain of smallpox – it would give them antibodies against the disease. It worked and today smallpox has practically been wiped out from the world as a result of widespread inoculations.

Although Jenner is the person best known for his work with smallpox, people had been experimenting with the idea of inoculation much earlier in the century. Lady Mary Wortley Montagu, married to the British Ambassador to Istanbul, was fascinated by the Turkish attitude to smallpox. Above, you can read her description of the Turkish method of inoculating people against the deadly disease. This letter was written in 1717, nearly eighty years before Jenner's breakthrough.

> *'The smallpox, so fatal and so general amongst us, is here entirely harmless by the invention of engrafting ....They make parties for this purpose and when they are met (commonly fifteen or sixteen together) the old woman comes with a nutshell full of the matter of the best sort of smallpox and asks what veins you please to have opened. She immediately rips open that you offer to her with a large needle (which gives you no more pain than a common scratch) and puts into the vein as much venom as can lie upon the head of her needle, and after binds up the little wound with a hollow bit of shell.'*
>
> **From the diaries of Lady Montagu**

Lady Mary added that she would have written and promoted the idea with doctors in England but she obviously didn't have a very high opinion of the medical profession. She suspected they would rather make money through tending to all the smallpox victims than get rid of the disease.

After inoculating with cowpox

Out damned spot!

Smallpox often scarred people terribly and velvet patches were worn by both men and women to hide the worst scars.

A Tale of Two Clerics

This is the tale of two very different men who were clergymen in the Church of England: John Wesley, the founder of Methodism and Frederick Hervey, the Bishop of Derry in Northern Ireland.

John Wesley

John Wesley was a Church of England parson who had a religious experience in 1738 when he suddenly realised that God loved him and that he was 'saved'. He then felt it his duty to communicate his message and for the next fifty-three years he worked tirelessly around England and Wales, covering more than 250,000 miles on horseback and preaching more than 40,000 sermons. Many of his sermons were given in the open air to the inhabitants of the mining villages and new towns which had sprung up as a result of the industrial revolution.

Wesley preached that all men were equal spiritually but this was not popular with the upper classes who were afraid that it would encourage the lower classes to rise up against them. This was the view of Methodism from one member of the aristocracy, the Duchess of Buckingham:

'their doctrines [theories] *are most repulsive, and strongly tinctured* [flavoured] *with impertinence and disrespect towards their superiors, in perpetually endeavouring to level all ranks and to do away with all distinctions, as it is monstrous to be told that you have a heart as sinful as the common wretches that crawl on the earth'.*

Wesley also had strong feelings about decency and was not impressed by some features of the new landscape gardens at Stourhead in Wiltshire. This is what he wrote in his Journal after his visit in 1776:

'I have seen the most celebrated gardens in England but these far exceed them all. Others were delighted with the temples, but I was not (1) because several of the statues about them were mean; (2) because I cannot admire the images of devils – and we know the gods of the heathen are but devils; (3) because I defy all mankind to reconcile statues with nudities either to common sense or common decency.'

Wesley had always intended his followers, who became known as Methodists, to remain part of the Church of England but after his death in 1791 it was clear that the differences were too great and the one million Methodists in England and Wales split from the Anglicans.

Frederick was an eccentric character and loved his new position of authority. He started huge building projects in his diocese (the area he controlled), including a bridge over the River Foyle, restoration work to the cathedral, and road building, as well as several grand houses for himself. He made a point of visiting all the parsons in the diocese to make sure that their living conditions were satisfactory. One of his most popular moves among the Irish was to swear that he would never appoint an Englishman to any of the parishes in his area. Although Hervey introduced many improvements to the diocese not many of them were really to do with religion.

> 'My rides in a morning are of five and six hours among the tombs of Heros, the Palaces of Emperors and spoils of the Universe, for miles together you discover Aqueducts, temples, Pillars, etc. all that can recall the view of Rome from whence all originated, and to which all tended, fills the eye with all that is magnificent and the mind with all that is aweful' [breathtaking].

Frederick Hervey

In comparison to John Wesley's Methodism with all its high principles, the Church of England had become rather corrupt by the eighteenth century. As a rule, the people controlling it were more concerned with wealth, money and power rather than spreading a religious message. Getting a well-paid and respected post in the Church of England was really down to who you knew, not necessarily how good a Christian you were.

Frederick Hervey, Bishop of Derry in Northern Ireland from 1768 to 1803, was a case in point. He was one of the younger sons of a well-known aristocratic family and was lucky in that his elder brother was appointed Lord Lieutenant of Ireland. As a result of his influence he was appointed Bishop of Derry in 1768, a post which could earn him more than £20,000 a year in rents and fines.

Although Frederick enjoyed an extravagant lifestyle in Derry, his great love was travelling abroad. While Wesley covered miles in Britain collecting converts, Hervey spent years travelling around Europe collecting works of art. In 1779 he inherited the family title and became the 4th Earl of Bristol. He found himself with an income of £40,000 a year – a great amount of money. Like many high-ranking clergy Hervey didn't feel that he had a duty to stay in his diocese and for the last eleven years of his life he didn't set foot in Derry. Hervey adored life in Italy, and unlike Wesley, he obviously couldn't see anything wrong in temples or nude statues! This is his description of how he passed a typical morning

Frederick Hervey died suddenly in 1803 in Italy. His body was shipped back to England in a box labelled 'Antique Statue', as sailors were very superstitious about carrying bodies on board ship.

Hervey had a wicked sense of humour and once invited some of the more overweight members of his clergy over to a huge dinner to discuss who should take over a profitable post in the diocese that had fallen vacant. After they had stuffed their faces Frederick announced that it would be decided on the outcome of a running race and set them off waddling through a very muddy course; all of them became so bogged down that no one reached the finishing line and Frederick chose someone else to fill the post!

Hervey also had a flamboyant style of dress:

'the eccentric Earl-Bishop rides about the streets of Rome dressed in red plush breeches and a broad-brimmed white or straw hat, and was often asked if that was the canonical costume of an Irish prelate'.

Clothes and Fashion

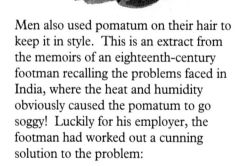

The first half of the eighteenth century saw some excessive styles in personal fashion. This was the comment of one man seeing two women trying to pass each other in a room:

> 'I have been in a moderate large room where there had been but two ladies who had not space to move without lifting up their petticoats higher than their grandmothers would have thought decent'
>
> **Universal Spectator – January 1741**

These dresses were often works of engineering and some of the wider pannier dresses fashionable in the 1740s incorporated hinges so that the wearer wouldn't get stuck! The writer had obviously been watching a pre-hinge model ...

Lazy lace

Lace was considered a luxury and sign of wealth and status. A man wearing dangling lace cuffs gave the impression to anyone who saw him that he never had to worry about getting his hands or cuffs dirty and so never had to do labouring work.

Sense at last

In the latter part of the eighteenth century the craze for all things classical also spread to dress. Women were freed from wearing huge skirts and instead they adopted high-waisted, loosely flowing dresses similar to Roman dress.

Hair-raising problems

The hairstyles of the 1770s and 1780s were notoriously extravagant. It was not unheard of for women to sport hairstyles built up over a wire frame up to 2 metres in height! This construction was plastered with a mixture of apple pressings and hog grease (called pomatum) to make it firm and sticky, then covered in powder. Although these hairstyles must have looked very impressive, they were very difficult to keep, especially as the smell of the pomatum attracted mice and insects and so the hairstyle needed to be de-infested regularly!

Men also used pomatum on their hair to keep it in style. This is an extract from the memoirs of an eighteenth-century footman recalling the problems faced in India, where the heat and humidity obviously caused the pomatum to go soggy! Luckily for his employer, the footman had worked out a cunning solution to the problem:

> 'When the Colonel came home, he said: 'John, my hair stands up as well as when I went out, and all the other gentlemen's hair is down.' I said: 'Sir, the people here don't know how to use the pomade'; for I had contrived to stiffen the pomatum with waxen candles.'
>
> **Memoirs of an Eighteenth-Century Footman**

Babies and children

In Tudor and Stuart times children were treated as mini adults, but during the eighteenth century it was accepted that children needed toys and more suitable clothes for play. The practice of swaddling (tightly bandaging) babies at birth to make their limbs grow straight, was now questioned. This is the advice given in a book on child care written by Dr William Cadogan which was bought by Sir Matthew Fetherstonhaugh of Uppark in Sussex before the birth of his son, Harry, in 1754. The doctor suggested:

'laying aside all those Swathes, Bandages, Stays, and Contrivances, that are most ridiculously used to close and keep the Head in its Place and support the Body. As if Nature, exact Nature, had produced her chief Work, a human Creature, so carelessly unfinished as to want [need] those Idle Aids to make it perfect. Shoes and Stockings are very needless Incumbrances, besides that they keep the Legs wet and nasty ... a child would stand firmer and learn to walk much sooner without them ...'

Too much or too little hair?

High hair lines were considered fashionable and people were prepared to go through a very unpleasant process in order to achieve a high forehead. They would pluck out the hair and then plaster the forehead with cat dung and vinegar. But those who had lost too much hair plastered bear grease on their scalp as a restorer.

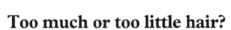

Make a Georgian mask

Masquerades were balls where the guests wore masks for at least the first half of the evening. The intention was to disguise yourself and masks were often very elaborate using jewels and feathers. They would always cover the eye area if not the whole face. Have a go at designing your own Georgian mask. Draw the outline of your mask on a piece of card (here are a few shapes to give you a starting point), cut out eye holes and decorate it. Then tape the back of one side of it to a thin baton of wood about 30cm long and you are ready for your first masked ball!

Places to Visit

A selection of National Trust Properties with eighteenth-century links

Georgian cotton mill (p.8):

Quarry Bank Mill, Cheshire

Fine Georgian/Queen Anne town houses (p.10):

Peckover, Wisbech

Mompesson, Salisbury

Carlyle's House, Cheyne Walk, London

Fenton House in Hampstead, and Rainham Hall in Essex are examples of houses built by merchants aiming to escape London's busy and rapidly-developing centre.

Example of the Georgian town social scene (p.10):

Bath Assembly Rooms, Avon

Home of the Parminster sisters (p.12):

A la Ronde, Devon, with examples of shellwork and featherwork.

Family seat of Admiral George Anson (p.14):

Shugborough, Staffordshire

Houses designed or altered by Robert Adam (p.18):

Kedleston Hall, Derbyshire

Osterley Park, Middlesex

Hatchlands Park, Surrey

Nostell Priory, Yorkshire

Architects who worked in the classical style (p.18):

Asprucci	Ickworth, Suffolk
Campbell	Stourhead, Wiltshire
Carr	Basildon Park, Berkshire
Gibbs	Antony, Cornwall Wimpole, Cambridgeshire
Holland	Berrington Hall, Hereford & Worcester
Leoni	Clandon, Surrey Lyme Park, Cheshire
Robinson	Claydon, Bucks
Steuart	Attingham, Shropshire
Stuart	Shugborough, Staffs
Talman	Dyrham Park, Avon
Samuel Wyatt	Tatton, Cheshire
James Wyatt	Castle Coole, Northern Ireland

Eighteenth-century landscape gardens (p.20):

Claremont, Surrey

Stowe, Buckinghamshire

Studley Royal, Yorkshire

Stourhead, Wiltshire

West Wycombe Park, Buckinghamshire

Rievaulx Terrace and Temples, Yorkshire

'Grand Tourists' (p.22):

William Windham
Felbrigg, Norfolk

Henry Hoare II
Stourhead, Wiltshire

George Lucy
Charlecote, Warwickshire

Sir Matthew Fetherstonehaugh
Uppark, Sussex (See p.26 & p.31)

Connections with the artist, Sir Joshua Reynolds (p.22):

Saltram, Devon

Fine collections of portraits by other leading painters can be seen at (p.22):

Kingston Lacy, Dorset

Knole, Kent

Petworth, Sussex

Waddesdon, Bucks

Georgian charity schools (p.24):

Blewcoat School, Victoria, London

Sutton House, Hackney, London

Chapels (p.28):

Ickworth, Suffolk and
Mussenden Temple, Co. Londonderry

Built by Frederick Hervey, Bishop of Derry and 4th Earl of Bristol

Also at:

Erddig, Clwyd

Gibside, Tyne & Wear

Wimpole, Cambridgeshire

Georgian kitchens (p.26):

Erddig, Clwyd

Kedleston, Derbyshire

Saltram, Devon

'Service' rooms (p.26):

Charlecote, Warwickshire	*Brewhouse*
Erddig, Clwyd	*Bakery*
Shugborough, Staffs	*Dairy, Bakery*
Uppark, Hampshire	*Dairy*

Fine collections of costumes (p.30):

Spring Hill, Northern Ireland

Killerton, Devon

Sizergh, Cumbria

Portraits displaying eighteenth century costumes (p.30):

Beningbrough, York

Calke, Derbyshire

Erddig, Clwyd

Saltram, Devon

First published in 1995 by National Trust (Enterprises) Ltd, 36 Queen Anne's Gate, London SW1H 9AS

Registered Charity No. 205846

Copyright © The National Trust 1995

ISBN: 0 7078 0196 6

Designed by Blade Communications, Leamington Spa

Printed by Wing King Tong Ltd., Hong Kong